I0782728

Instant Happiness Quotes

100 Powerful Thoughts to Empower Self-Confidence, Cultivate Resilience, and Illuminate the Path to Joyful Living.

www.dipaali.life

COPYRIGHT@2024 BY DIPAALI PATEL

All rights reserved. No part of this book may be reproduced in any form without permission in writing from the author. No part of this publication may be reproduced or transmitted in any form or by any means, mechanical or electronic, including photocopying, or recording, or by any information storage and retrieval system, or transmitted by email or by any other means whatsoever without permission in writing from the author.

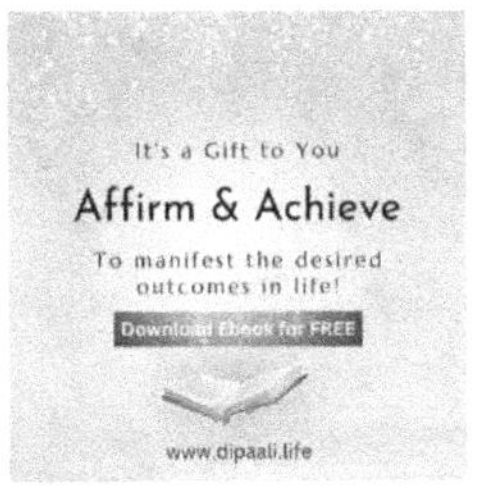

Our thoughts and words shape our reality, so it's essential to monitor and transform any negative thoughts before expressing them. Spoken words possess the power to change our destiny. By downloading a free e-book, you can access a list of empowering affirmations designed to counteract negative self-talk. Practicing these affirmations daily, along with utilizing nine manifestation secrets, can help you achieve desired outcomes in all areas of your life.

Click here to download eBook for free

DEDICATION

For those seeking to open any page of this book and shift their perspective from a sense of lack to a mindset of abundance.

TABLE OF CONTENTS

DOWNLOAD E-BOOK FOR FREE.............III
100 QUOTES & WISDOM WORDS..............5
ABOUT AUTHOR 107
MY BOOKS 109
BIG ASK 115

Introduction

We need a quick dose of motivation daily to be happy and productive in life, despite investing exclusive time for personal transformation.

Here are 100 powerful quotes that can instantly bring you happiness. As you read these positive statements, your mindset will shift, allowing you to let go of anger and stress. In turn, your confidence will grow, replacing any fear you may have.

Keep some ideas or questions in mind as you open this book. Flip to any page and choose a quote of the day. By reading that quote, you may just magically find the answer. Not only should you read this book at least once in your lifetime or within the next 100 days, but you can also flip to any page of this book at any time and find the solution to your problem to that time.

Connect with your current life situation and uncover the hidden message of the universe through this quote. Believe in your guiding angels, and they will assist you in navigating through life's storms.

Incorporate the habit of perceiving the positive aspects in difficult situations or with challenging individuals. Adopt a broader perspective when facing problems and make an effort to extract valuable lessons from them, utilizing quotes for inspiration. Strive to attain a lifelong state of happiness by nurturing wisdom through the insightful words contained in each quote.

This book aims to bring you instant happiness and help you maintain it for a longtime. It empowers you to overcome fear, anxiety, and stress, and encourages self-love. Through reading, you will gain a deeper understanding of your self-worth, while dramatically increasing your confidence and ability to make effective decisions.

I have marked my favorite quotes with a little star as they have had a profound impact on my life. Please share yours when you write your review for this book.

I hope you find lasting happiness in every situation life presents.

100 Quotes & Wisdom Words

#1 ☆

God's way is better than your way.
His plan is bigger than your plan. His
dream of your life is more rewarding,
mor fulfilling, better than you have
ever dreamed of. Now stay open and
let God do it his way.

– Joel Osteen

WISDOM WORDS 1

This quote encapsulates the essence of surrendering to a higher power. It speaks to the idea that relinquishing control and trusting in something greater than ourselves often leads to outcomes surpassing our wildest expectations. By embracing humility and openness, we invite divine guidance into our lives, allowing for a journey that exceeds our limited human understanding and ultimately leads to greater fulfillment and purpose.

#2 ☆

---

*Whatever happened was good.
What's happening is going well.
Whatever will happen will also
be good. Don't worry about the
future. Live in the present.*

– Lord Krishna

WISDOM WORDS 2

This quote embodies the essence of acceptance and mindfulness. It teaches us to trust in the inherent goodness of life's unfolding, even amidst challenges. By letting go of worries about the future and focusing on the present moment, we cultivate peace and resilience. Embracing each moment with gratitude and awareness allows us to find joy and contentment regardless of circumstances, recognizing that life's journey is ultimately guided by a higher wisdom.

#3

Someday, everything will make perfect sense. So, for now, laugh at the confusion, smile through the tears, be strong and keep reminding yourself that everything happens for a reason.

- John Mayer

WISDOM WORDS 3

This statement encourages perseverance amidst confusion and hardship, trusting that clarity will emerge in due time. By finding humor in chaos, maintaining optimism through adversity, and believing in the underlying purpose of life's twists and turns, we navigate challenges with grace.

#4 ☆

Life has many different chapters, don't let one bad chapter end the book.

\- *Gautam Buddha.*

WISDOM WORDS 4

Wisdom is understanding that setbacks are just temporary chapters in life's larger narrative. This statement urges resilience in the face of adversity, reminding us not to let isolated hardships define our entire journey. Embracing change and growth, we recognize that each chapter contributes to the richness and depth of our life story.

#5

---

*If you can do something
about a situation, why
worry? And if you can't do
something about a situation,
why worry?*

- *Dalai Lama*

WISDOM WORDS 5

This quote encapsulates the essence of wisdom by highlighting the futility of worry. It reminds us to focus our energy on constructive action, when possible, rather than dwelling on what we cannot change. Embracing this mindset fosters peace and resilience, allowing us to navigate life's challenges with a calm and empowered perspective.

#6 

---

*If it's out of your hands, it
deserves freedom from your
mind too.*

- Ivan Nuru

WISDOM WORDS 6

True wisdom lies in recognizing the limits of control. This quote emphasizes the importance of letting go of worry and obsession over things beyond our influence. By releasing attachment to outcomes beyond our control, we free our minds from unnecessary burdens, allowing for greater peace, acceptance, and focus on what we can change.

#7

*Why worry? If you have
done the very best you can,
worrying won't make it any
better.*

- *Walt Disney*

WISDOM WORDS 7

Wisdom lies in accepting the limits of our control. If we've given our best effort, worrying becomes futile. Instead, focus on what's within our power, trusting that outcomes are shaped by our actions. Redirecting energy from worry to proactive steps fosters resilience and peace, allowing us to navigate challenges with clarity and confidence.

#8 ☆

Life is about accepting the challenges along the way, choosing to keep moving forward, and savoring the journey.

- Roy T. Bennett

WISDOM WORDS 8

Wisdom lies in embracing life's challenges as opportunities for growth. It's about persisting through adversity, refusing to be hindered by setbacks, and finding joy in the journey itself. By choosing to move forward with courage and resilience, we discover the true essence of living and uncover the beauty in every step of the way.

#9

Life is a series of natural and spontaneous changes. Don't resist them; that only creates sorrow. Let reality be reality. Let things flow naturally forward in whatever way they like.

- Lao Tzu

WISDOM WORDS 9

Wisdom lies in accepting the ebb and flow of life's constant changes. Resisting this natural rhythm leads to unnecessary suffering. Instead, embrace reality as it unfolds, allowing events to progress organically. By relinquishing control and flowing with life's currents, we find peace and harmony, adapting to each twist and turn with grace and resilience.

#10 

*In the end, it's not the years
in your life that count. It's
the life in your years.*

- Abraham Lincoln

WISDOM WORDS 10

True wisdom lies in prioritizing the quality of experiences over mere quantity of time. This quote underscores the importance of living fully and meaningfully, regardless of lifespan. Focusing on creating rich, fulfilling moments imbues our existence with depth and purpose, leaving a lasting legacy far beyond the measure of years alone.

#11 ☆

---

*The greatness of man is not
how much wealth he acquires,
but in his integrity and his
ability to affect those around
him positively.*

- Bob Marley

WISDOM WORDS 11

True greatness resides in the character and impact of an individual, not merely in material wealth. It's reflected in one's integrity, moral principles, and the positive influence they exert on others. Wealth may come and go, but the enduring legacy of kindness, compassion, and ethical behavior leaves an indelible mark on humanity's collective journey.

#12

---

*If you feel like you are losing
everything remember trees lose
their leaves every year, and
they stand tall and wait for
better days to come.*

- Unknown

WISDOM WORDS 12

---

*This quote illustrates the resilience found in
nature, offering a powerful metaphor for
enduring difficult times. Like trees shedding
leaves in preparation for renewal, we too can let
go of burdens and trust in the cyclical nature of
life. By remaining steadfast in hope, we can
weather adversity and anticipate brighter days
ahead.*

#13 

It's not the load that break you down, it's the way you carry it.

- *Lou Holtz*

WISDOM WORDS 13

Wisdom lies in understanding that the weight of life's challenges doesn't determine our fate; rather, it's our attitude and approach that shape our resilience. By embracing adversity with strength, optimism, and adaptability, we can carry even the heaviest burdens with grace and emerge stronger on the other side.

#14

One of the simplest way to stay happy is letting go of the things that makes you sad.

- Unknown

WISDOM WORDS 14

True happiness often springs from releasing burdens that weigh us down. Letting go of sadness frees us from its grip, allowing space for joy to enter our lives. Embracing this simplicity empowers us to focus on what truly uplifts us, fostering a brighter and more fulfilling existence.

#15

*Happiness is the choice that
requires effort at times.*

- Aeschylus

WISDOM WORDS 15

Wisdom lies in recognizing that happiness is not merely a fleeting emotion but a conscious decision we make each day. It requires effort to cultivate positivity, gratitude, and resilience, especially during challenging times. By choosing happiness despite obstacles, we empower ourselves to find joy and fulfillment in every moment of our lives.

#16

5 steps to happiness

*- Smile more, - Worry less, -
Be present, - Give more, -
Expect less*

- Gautam Buddha

WISDOM WORDS 16

True happiness stems from simplicity and mindfulness. These steps advocate for a balanced approach to life: smiling to spread joy, reducing worry to foster peace, staying present to appreciate each moment fully, giving generously to cultivate fulfillment, and expecting less to embrace contentment regardless of outcomes.

#17 ☆

---

*You don't have to have a
reason to feel good – You are
alive; You can feel good for
no reason at all.*

- *Tony Robbins*

WISDOM WORDS 17

True wisdom lies in recognizing the inherent joy of simply being alive. You don't always need a specific reason to feel good; the mere fact of existence is cause enough. Embrace the present moment, find gratitude in the smallest of things, and let the sheer experience of life be your reason for happiness.

#18 ☆

---

*All is well. Everything is
working out for my highest
good. Out of this situation,
only good will come.*

I am safe.

\- *Louise Hay*

WISDOM WORDS 18

*This affirmation embodies the power of positive
thinking and trust in the universe. By affirming
that all is well, and everything is working for
one's highest good, it cultivates a mindset of
resilience and faith. It reminds us to see
challenges as opportunities for growth and to
believe in our inherent safety and well-being.*

#19 ☆

Never let a day pass without looking for the good, feeling the good withing you, praising, appreciating, blessings and being grateful. Make it your life commitment, and you will stand in utter awe of what happens in your life.

- Rhonda Byrne

WISDOM WORDS 19

Wisdom is found in daily gratitude and appreciation. By actively seeking and acknowledging the goodness within and around us, we cultivate a mindset of abundance and joy. Making gratitude a lifelong practice transforms our perspective, inviting more blessings and miracles into our lives, leaving us awestruck by the beauty and abundance that unfolds each day.

#20 ☆

Hack your path with forgiveness. Hack your present with mindfulness. Hack your future with

"I AM ENOUGH.

- Unknown

WISDOM WORDS 20

Wisdom lies in the transformative power of forgiveness, allowing us to release the burdens of the past and forge a brighter path. Mindfulness in the present brings clarity and peace, enabling us to navigate challenges with grace. Affirming "I AM ENOUGH" empowers us to shape a future rooted in self-worth and authenticity, fostering fulfillment and resilience.

#21

*Move out of your comfort zone.
You can only grow if you are
willing to feel awkward and
uncomfortable when you try
something new.*

- Brian Tracy

WISDOM WORDS 21

Wisdom lies in embracing discomfort as a catalyst for growth. Stepping beyond familiarity fosters personal development and resilience. By challenging ourselves to explore the unknown and endure discomfort, we expand our capabilities and unlock new potentials. In these moments of unease, we discover the true extent of our strength and adaptability.

#22

You future is created by what you do today, not tomorrow.

- Robert Kiyosaki

WISDOM WORDS 22

Wisdom underscores the power of present actions in shaping future outcomes. This quote emphasizes seizing the opportunity of today, as it directly influences the trajectory of tomorrow. By prioritizing proactive steps and mindful choices in the present moment, we actively mold the path towards our desired future, unlocking its potential through intentional deeds.

#23 

The best investment you can make, is an investment in yourself.....

The more you learn, the more you will earn.

- Warren buffet

WISDOM WORDS 23

Investing in oneself yields the highest returns. By prioritizing self-improvement and continuous learning, one enhances their skills, knowledge, and capabilities. This not only enriches personal growth and fulfillment but also opens doors to greater opportunities and financial rewards. Education and self-development are invaluable assets that fuel success and prosperity in all aspects of life.

#24 

Don't be a victim of negative self-talk. Remember you are listening.

- Bob Proctor

WISDOM WORDS 24

Wisdom lies in recognizing the power of our internal dialogue. Refusing to succumb to self-defeating thoughts, we reclaim control over our mindset. By actively monitoring and challenging negative self-talk, we empower ourselves to cultivate a more positive and supportive inner narrative. Remember, we are both the speaker and the listener in this conversation with ourselves.

#25

Your time is limited, so don't waste it living someone else's life.

- Steve jobs

WISDOM WORDS 25

Wisdom lies in recognizing the preciousness of time and honoring one's unique journey. This quote reminds us to prioritize authenticity and purpose, rather than conforming to others' expectations. By embracing our individual paths and passions, we maximize the value of our limited time, living with intention and fulfillment.

#26

Happiness is when what you think, what you say, and what you do are in harmony.

- Mahatma Gandhi

WISDOM WORDS 26

True happiness arises from alignment between thoughts, words, and actions. When our inner thoughts, spoken words, and deeds are congruent, we experience a profound sense of contentment and peace. This harmony fosters authenticity, integrity, and a deeper connection with oneself and the world, leading to lasting fulfillment and joy.

#27 ☆

If you want to be sad, no one in the world can make you happy. But if you make up your mind to be happy, no one and nothing on earth can take that happiness from you.

\- Paramahansa Yogananada

WISDOM WORDS 27

This quote underscores the power of personal choice and mindset in shaping our happiness. True contentment comes from within, independent of external circumstances or influences. By consciously deciding to cultivate joy and positivity, we reclaim control over our emotional state, ensuring that our happiness remains resilient and unwavering, regardless of external factors.

#28

---

*We have more faith in what
we imitate than in what we
originate.*

- Bruce Lee

WISDOM WORDS 28

---

*This quote underscores the power of emulation
over innovation. It suggests that humans often
place greater trust in what they observe and
replicate from others rather than creating
something original. It speaks to the influence of
social learning and the tendency to follow
established patterns rather than forging new
paths.*

#29

To truly laugh, you must be able to take your pain, and play with it.

- Charlie Chaplin

WISDOM WORDS 29

True laughter emerges from a deep understanding of life's complexities. It's about transforming pain into resilience, finding humor in adversity, and reclaiming joy despite challenges. By embracing our struggles with courage and lightness, we cultivate a profound sense of liberation and authenticity, allowing laughter to become a healing force in our lives.

#30 ☆

When nobody else celebrates you, learn to celebrate yourself. when nobody else compliment you, then compliment yourself. It's not up to other people to keep you encouraged. It's up to you.

- Jay Shetty

WISDOM WORDS 30

Wisdom teaches self-validation and resilience. Celebrating oneself and acknowledging personal worth independently of external validation fosters inner strength and confidence. Relying on one's own encouragement cultivates self-reliance and empowers individuals to navigate life's challenges with unwavering self-assurance.

#31 ☆

Who and what are we willing to give up in the pursuit of simplifying our life so that we can focus our finite amount of energy towards our priorities that are defined by our purpose in life

---

- Dandapani

WISDOM WORDS 31

True wisdom lies in discerning what truly matters and aligning our actions with our deepest purpose. It requires letting go of distractions and non-essential commitments to concentrate our energy on what brings fulfillment and meaning. Simplifying life enables us to invest fully in pursuits that resonate with our core values and aspirations.

#32

*Fear is a habit; so is self-pity,
defeat, anxiety, despair,
hopelessness, and resignation.
You can eliminate all of these
negative habits with two simple
resolves: I can and I will.*

- Napoleon Hill

WISDOM WORDS 32

Wisdom lies in recognizing that negative emotions are habitual patterns that can be overcome with determination. By embracing the empowering mindset of "I can and I will," one can break free from the cycle of fear, self-pity, and defeat, transforming life with a renewed sense of resilience, optimism, and agency.

#33 ☆

Acceptance doesn't mean person or scene is perfect and I let them be the way they are. Acceptance means that my mind doesn't get affected by the way they are. I change what I can change and bless what I can't.

- *Sister Shivani*

WISDOM WORDS 33

Wisdom lies in understanding the distinction between acceptance and passivity. It's about acknowledging imperfections without allowing them to disturb inner peace. Acceptance empowers us to focus on what's within our control, while gracefully embracing what isn't. By cultivating a mindset of gratitude and resilience, we navigate life's challenges with equanimity and compassion.

#34

Loosing something can really be a win. When you have lost an item, perhaps it was not to be supposed to be in your life anymore and the universe is telling you that you are ready for something new and better.

- Marie diamond

WISDOM WORDS 34

Wisdom recognizes that loss often paves the way for new beginnings. Losing something can signify outgrowing its place in our lives, signaling readiness for fresh opportunities. Viewing loss as a catalyst for growth allows us to embrace change with optimism, trusting that the universe guides us towards greater fulfillment and alignment with our true path.

#35

Look at every experience where you hearing people from different prospective as an opportunity to grow and learn.

- Jessica Berman

WISDOM WORDS 35

Wisdom flourishes when we approach interactions with openness and receptivity. Viewing encounters from diverse perspectives enriches understanding and fosters personal growth. Embracing each experience as a chance to broaden our horizons, we cultivate empathy, expand our worldview, and deepen our connection with others, nurturing continual learning and evolution.

#36 

---

*It always seems impossible
until it's done.*

- Nelson mandela

WISDOM WORDS 36

This quote encapsulates the essence of perseverance and belief in one's abilities. It reminds us that daunting tasks often appear insurmountable at first glance. However, with determination, effort, and resilience, what initially seems impossible can be achieved. It underscores the power of persistence and the triumph of human spirit over adversity.

#37 ☆

If you are insecure, guess what? The rest of the world is too. Don't overestimate the competition and underestimate yourself. You are better than you think.

- *T. Harv Eker*

WISDOM WORDS 37

Wisdom teaches us that insecurity is universal. Instead of being intimidated by perceived competition, recognize your inherent worth. Comparisons often distort reality. Trust in your abilities, for they are more substantial than you realize. Embrace authenticity, knowing that self-belief can propel you beyond perceived limitations, illuminating your unique path to success.

#38

---

*The future is not there
waiting for us. We create it
by the power of imagination.*

- Pir Vilayat Khan

WISDOM WORDS 38

---

*This quote underscores the creative potential of
the human mind. It reminds us that the future is
not predetermined but shaped by our thoughts,
intentions, and actions. Through the power of
imagination, we envision possibilities and
manifest our desired outcomes, actively shaping
the course of our lives and the world around us.*

#39

So much that was beautiful and so much that was hard to bear. Yet whenever I showed myself ready to bear it, the hard was directly transformed into beautiful.

- Etty Hillesum

WISDOM WORDS 39

This quote highlights the transformative power of resilience and readiness to embrace life's challenges. By facing difficulties with courage and acceptance, we catalyze their metamorphosis into sources of beauty and growth. It speaks to the profound shift that occurs when we approach adversity with an open heart and a willingness to learn and evolve.

#40 

The trouble with happiness is people don't practice it.

- Paul Mckenna

WISDOM WORDS 40

This quote highlights the paradox of happiness: its simplicity and elusiveness. True happiness often eludes us because we overlook the importance of practicing gratitude, mindfulness, and self-care. By actively cultivating happiness through daily habits and positive mindset shifts, we can overcome the tendency to take it for granted and experience its abundance.

#41 ☆

The deepest secret is that life is not process of discovery, but a process of creation. You are not discovering yourself, but creating yourself anew. Seek therefor, not to find out who you are, but seek to determine who you want to be.

- Neale Donald Walsch

WISDOM WORDS 41

True wisdom lies in realizing that life is not about uncovering a predetermined identity, but rather about actively shaping and reinventing oneself. By embracing the power of creation, we shift our focus from passive discovery to intentional self-definition. Rather than seeking to uncover a fixed truth, we empower ourselves to consciously craft the person we aspire to become.

#42 

*If you really want to perform
at your best, everything has
to be fully aligned.*

- Steven Kotler

WISDOM WORDS 42

True excellence stems from alignment—when your thoughts, actions, and intentions harmonize seamlessly. To perform at your peak, cultivate coherence in your goals, values, and behaviors. This holistic alignment fosters focus, clarity, and effectiveness, propelling you towards your highest potential with purpose and conviction.

#43

As you embrace your deepest nature, the energies of your being shine forth into your body, your mind and your world.

- Donna Eden

Wisdom Words 43

Embracing one's true essence ignites a transformative energy that permeates every aspect of existence. By aligning with our deepest nature, we illuminate our body, mind, and surroundings with authenticity and vitality. This profound self-acceptance radiates outward, fostering harmony within ourselves and resonating positively with the world around us.

#44 ☆

It's your responsibility to show the world how to treat you by the way in which you treat yourself.

- Lisa Nichols

WISDOME WORDS 44

This quote underscores the power of self-respect and self-care in shaping external interactions. By valuing and treating ourselves with kindness, respect, and dignity, we set a standard for how others should treat us. Our self-perception influences the dynamics of all relationships, emphasizing the importance of cultivating a positive and nurturing relationship with ourselves.

#45 ☆

It's about consistent effort you bring every single day that lead to small incremental improvement. Little by little. A little becomes a lot. Don't complicate it. Keep it simple. Ignore the noise. Work hard, keep learning. Be kind. Amazing things will happen.

- Jim Kwik

WISDOM WORDS 45

Wisdom lies in the power of daily commitment and incremental progress. By consistently applying effort and focusing on small improvements, we pave the path to success. Simplify the process, stay resilient amidst distractions, and prioritize hard work and continuous learning. Through kindness and perseverance, we create the foundation for remarkable achievements to unfold.

#46 

The greatest discovery of all time is that a person can change their future by merely changing their ATTITUDE.

- Oprah Winfrey

WISDOM WORDS 46

Wisdom lies in realizing the transformative power of attitude. By shifting our perspective, we reshape our reality and influence our future. Embracing positivity, resilience, and gratitude can propel us toward greater fulfillment and success. Through this understanding, we harness the ability to navigate life's challenges with optimism and create our own paths to happiness.

#47 

Once your way of being consciously chosen, you become the creator of your own destiny.

- Sadhguru

WISDOM WORDS 47

Wisdom lies in the power of intentional choices. When we consciously shape our attitudes, actions, and beliefs, we reclaim agency over our lives. By aligning our way of being with our deepest values and aspirations, we unleash our potential as creators of our destiny, shaping a path guided by purpose and fulfillment.

#48

---

*People who appreciate life
are more liked, more
approachable, and more
attractive. As a result they
invite all kind of
opportunities into their lives.*

- *Ken Honda*

WISDOM WORDS 48

Wisdom lies in the appreciation of life's beauty and blessings, fostering an aura of positivity and warmth. Such individuals radiate approachability and charm, drawing others towards them naturally. Their open-heartedness attracts a multitude of opportunities, as their gratitude and joy for life create an inviting magnetism that enriches their experiences and connections.

#49 

---

*Life is university, and you
never graduate. Accept that
whatever happens to you, no
matter how terrible, it is
there to teach you. Your job
is to learn and do what you
have to.*

- *Srikumar Rao*

WISDOM WORDS 49

*Life is an eternal classroom where every
experience, even the most challenging, offers
valuable lessons. Embrace the journey with an
open heart, recognizing that adversity is a
catalyst for growth. Your task is to glean wisdom
from every situation, evolving into a wiser and
more resilient version of yourself with each
lesson learned.*

#50

The great human problem of evil stems from the illusion of separateness. Whenever this illusion is overcome, we behave lovingly to one another.

- Barbara Marx Hubbard

WISDOM WORDS 50

Wisdom lies in recognizing the interconnectedness of all beings. The illusion of separateness fuels the human problem of evil, fostering division and conflict. Yet, when we transcend this illusion and acknowledge our inherent unity, compassion naturally emerges. By embracing love and understanding our shared humanity, we dissolve barriers and cultivate a world of kindness and harmony.

#51

The truth is not necessarily set you free, but truthfulness will.

- *Ken Wilber*

WISDOM WORDS 51

True freedom comes not solely from knowing the truth, but from living authentically in alignment with it. Embracing honesty cultivates inner peace and integrity, liberating us from the burden of deceit and self-delusion. By choosing truthfulness in thought, word, and action, we attain a profound sense of liberation and empowerment.

#52 

Your words make your reality. If you don't like your reality, change your WORDS.

- Marisa Peer

WISDOM WORDS 52

This quote emphasizes the power of language in shaping our experiences. Wisdom lies in understanding that our words are not just expressions but creators of our reality. By choosing positive, empowering language, we can transform our perception and ultimately influence the world we inhabit. Changing our words initiates a profound shift toward a more desirable reality.

#53 

Be happy with what you have while working for what you want.

- *Bob Hope*

WISDOM WORDS 53

True contentment arises from gratitude for the present moment, coupled with ambition for the future. This wisdom encourages appreciation for one's current blessings while maintaining the drive to pursue aspirations. Balancing satisfaction with striving fosters a harmonious mindset, where gratitude fuels progress, and each step forward is grounded in appreciation.

#54

*What are you becoming is
more important than what
are you accumulating.*

-   *Robin Sharma*

WISDOM WORDS 54

*True wisdom lies in the realization that personal
growth and character development hold more
significance than material possessions or
achievements. It emphasizes the importance of
cultivating virtues, integrity, and empathy, as
they shape who we are and how we impact the
world around us, transcending the fleeting value
of external wealth or success.*

#55 ☆

---

*One of greatest challenges in
changing habits is
maintaining awareness of
what we are actually doing.*

- James Clear

WISDOM WORDS 55

Wisdom reminds us that true transformation begins with conscious awareness. To change habits, we must first observe our actions without judgment. By cultivating mindfulness, we gain insight into our behaviors, allowing us to make intentional choices aligned with our goals. Awareness is the cornerstone of lasting change and personal growth.

#56

We are not perfect, forgive others as you would want to be forgiven.

- Catherine Pulsifer

WISDOM WORDS 56

Wisdom lies in recognizing our shared imperfections and embracing forgiveness as a transformative act. By extending the same grace to others that we desire for ourselves, we cultivate empathy, heal wounds, and nurture understanding. Forgiveness liberates us from resentment, fostering compassion and harmony in our relationships and within ourselves.

#57 

If you can't fly then run, if you can't run then walk, if you can't walk then crawl. But whatever you do, you have to keep moving forward.

- Martin Luther King Jr.

WISDOM WORDS 57

This quote embodies the essence of resilience and determination. It urges us to adapt to our circumstances and persevere, no matter how challenging the journey may seem. Whether flying, running, walking, or crawling, the key is to maintain forward momentum, embracing the process of growth and progress despite obstacles.

#58 

The purpose of our lives is to be happy.

- Dalai Lama

WISDOM WORDS 58

True wisdom lies in understanding that happiness is not merely a destination but a journey. It's about finding joy in the present moment, cultivating meaningful connections, pursuing passions, and living authentically. While happiness may fluctuate, embracing gratitude and purpose can lead to a fulfilling and contented life.

#59 

One ounce of practice is worth a thousand pounds of theory.

- Swami Vivekanand

WISDOM WORDS 59

This quote underscores the value of action over mere knowledge. Wisdom lies in the application of what we learn. While theory is important, practical experience carries greater weight. Through practice, we gain insight, skill, and a deeper understanding that surpasses theoretical knowledge alone, making it invaluable in achieving mastery and success.

#60

Yoga allows you to rediscover a sense of wholeness in your life, where you don't feel like you are constantly trying to feet broken pieces together.

- *B.K.S.Iyengar*

WISDOM WORDS 60

Wisdom lies in recognizing yoga's transformative power to cultivate inner harmony and integration. By aligning body, mind, and spirit, yoga fosters a profound sense of completeness, alleviating the need to mend fragmented aspects of oneself. Through its practice, individuals discover a holistic sense of well-being, embracing their entirety with acceptance and grace.

#61 

*Life is not worth living
unless it is lived for others.*

- Mother Teresa

WISDOM WORDS 61

True fulfillment in life is found in service to others. When we prioritize the well-being and happiness of those around us, our own existence gains profound meaning and purpose. Acts of kindness, empathy, and selflessness not only enrich the lives of others but also bring a deeper sense of fulfillment and interconnectedness to our own lives.

#62 ☆

In oneself lies the whole world and if you know how to look and learn, the door is there, and the key is in your hand. Nobody on earth can give you either key or the door to open, except yourself.

- Jiddu Krishnamurthi

WISDOM WORDS 62

This quote speaks to the power of self-awareness and personal responsibility. True fulfillment and understanding come from within; the world reflects our perceptions and interpretations. By learning to observe and introspect, we unlock boundless potential. The key to unlocking life's mysteries lies solely within ourselves; external sources can guide, but true enlightenment is self-discovered and self-actualized.

#63

*Everything in future will
improve if you are making a
spiritual effort now.*

- Swami Sri Yukteswar Giri

WISDOM WORDS 63

*The quote emphasizes the power of present
actions in shaping future outcomes, particularly
through spiritual endeavors. By investing in
spiritual growth and mindfulness today, one
cultivates a positive trajectory for the future. It
underscores the interconnectedness of inner work
and external circumstances, highlighting the
transformative potential of spiritual practice in
manifesting a brighter tomorrow.*

#64 ☆

None can destroy iron, but its own rust can! Likewise none can destroy a person, but it's own mindset can.

- Ratan Tata

WISDOM WORDS 64

This quote underscores the power of the mind in shaping our lives. Just as rust corrodes iron from within, our negative thoughts and beliefs can erode our well-being. Conversely, cultivating a resilient and positive mindset fortifies us against external challenges, enabling us to overcome obstacles and thrive amidst adversity.

#65

What we need to do is always lean into the future; when the world changes around you when it changes against you- what used to be tail wind is now a head wind. You have to lean into that and figure out what to do because complaining isn't a strategy.

\- *Jeff Bezos*

WISDOM WORDS 65

Wisdom entails adaptability and forward momentum. This quote emphasizes embracing change proactively, even when circumstances turn challenging. Rather than resisting, we must lean into adversity, seeking opportunities for growth and innovation. Complaining serves no purpose; instead, we must strategize and take decisive action to navigate shifting winds and shape our own destiny.

#66

Never give up. Today is hard, Tomorrow will be worse, but the day after tomorrow will be sunshine.

- *Jack Ma*

WISDOM WORDS 66

This quote embodies the essence of perseverance and hope. It reminds us that even in our darkest moments, brighter days lie ahead. By enduring today's challenges with resilience, we pave the way for a brighter tomorrow. Through steadfast determination and optimism, we find the strength to weather life's storms and embrace the sunshine awaiting us.

#67 

*In the end, you have to own
your mistakes and successes.*

- Dhirubhai Amabani

WISDOM WORDS 67

True wisdom comes from taking responsibility for both failures and achievements. Acknowledging mistakes fosters growth and humility, while recognizing successes instills confidence and gratitude. By owning our actions and their consequences, we gain valuable insights, learn from experiences, and ultimately shape our path towards personal fulfillment and success.

#68 

If there is a book that you want to read, but it hasn't been written yet, then you must write it.

- Toni Morrison

WISDOM WORDS 68

This quote embodies the essence of empowerment and creativity. It encourages us to take initiative and create the stories we wish to experience. By recognizing our own capacity to shape narratives and contribute to the world of literature, we fulfill our unique potential and enrich the collective human experience.

#69

*Anyone who has never made
a mistake has never tried
anything new.*

- Albert Einstein

WISDOM WORDS 69

This quote underscores the importance of embracing failure as a natural part of innovation and growth. Wisdom lies in understanding that mistakes are not indicators of incompetence but rather stepping stones to progress. By daring to venture into the unknown and learn from errors, we unlock new possibilities and expand our horizons.

#70 

Intelligent people tend to have less friends than the average person. The smarter you are, the more selective you become.

- Nikola Tesla

WISDOM WORDS 70

Wisdom reveals that intelligence often brings discernment in friendships. Smart individuals prioritize quality over quantity, choosing meaningful connections that align with their values and aspirations. As they value depth and intellectual stimulation, their circle may be smaller but richer, reflecting a deliberate choice for genuine bonds over superficial interactions.

#71

The cry we hear from deep in our hearts, comes from the wounded child within. Healing this inner child's pain is the key to transforming anger, sadness and fear.

- *Thich Nhat Hanh*

WISDOM WORDS 71

Wisdom lies in recognizing that unresolved childhood wounds often manifest as adult struggles. By acknowledging and tenderly healing our inner child's pain, we unlock profound transformation, transcending layers of anger, sadness, and fear. This journey of inner healing fosters emotional freedom and empowers us to live authentically and joyfully.

#72 

*Everything and everyone
around you is your
TEACHER.*

- Sai Reddy

WISDOM WORDS 72

Wisdom flourishes when we view every experience and encounter as an opportunity to learn. Embracing this mindset cultivates humility and openness, allowing us to glean wisdom from both positive and challenging situations, as well as from the diverse array of people we encounter. In this way, life becomes a continuous journey of growth and enlightenment.

#73

Every artist dips his brush into his own soul and paints his own nature into his art work. My art is self-discovery. I am creative energy in human form and my soul is my guide.

- *Unknown*

WISDOM WORDS 73

This quote illuminates the intimate connection between creativity and self-awareness. It embodies the wisdom that artistic expression is a journey of self-discovery, where the artist's innermost being is revealed through their creations. By embracing creativity as a means of exploring one's essence and allowing the soul to *guide, art becomes a profound vehicle for personal transformation.*

#74 ☆

The inner work never ends.
You are constantly evolving
into your higher self towards
endless levels of growth.

- Unknown

WISDOM WORDS 74

True wisdom recognizes that personal growth is a lifelong journey, not a destination. Embrace the continuous process of inner exploration and self-improvement. Each step forward unveils new layers of your being, leading you towards the fulfillment of your highest potential. Embrace the journey with openness and curiosity, for it is infinite and transformative.

#75 ☆

To love yourself right now, just as you are, is to give yourself heaven. Don't wait until you die. If you wait, you die now. If you love, you live now.

- Alan Cohen

WISDOM WORDS 75

Embrace self-love as the ultimate gift of liberation. By accepting yourself wholly in this moment, you unlock the joy and peace that transcend waiting for an uncertain future. Love breathes life into the present, offering a sanctuary of fulfillment. In loving yourself, you grant yourself the serenity of heaven, here and now.

#76 

To learn, you have to listen.
To improve, you have to try.

- Thomas Jefferson

WISDOM WORDS 76

True wisdom lies in the willingness to listen and the courage to act. Learning begins with attentive listening, absorbing insights from others and the world. Improvement comes from applying that knowledge, taking action despite uncertainty or fear. Embrace the cycle of listening and trying; it's the path to growth and mastery in any endeavor.

#77

*Our problems are man-
made, therefor they may be
solved by man. No problem
of human destiny is beyond
human beings.*

- John F Kennedy

WISDOM WORDS 77

This quote underscores human capability and responsibility in overcoming challenges. It reflects the wisdom that while humans create many of their own problems, they also possess the ingenuity and resilience to address them. It emphasizes the power of collective effort and innovation in shaping our destiny, instilling hope and empowerment

#78 

---

*Happiness can be found,
even in the darkest of times,
if one only remembers to
turn on the light.*

- Unknown

WISDOM WORDS 78

This quote underscores the power of perspective and resilience. It speaks to the human capacity to find light amidst darkness by consciously choosing hope and positivity. Despite life's challenges, happiness is attainable through the intentional decision to seek out brightness, even in the bleakest moments, illuminating the path forward with inner strength and optimism.

#79

*However difficult life may
seem, there is always
something you can do and
succeed at.*

- *Stephen Hawking*

WISDOM WORDS 79

Wisdom lies in recognizing the power of resilience and possibility within adversity. Even amidst challenges, opportunities for success abound. By focusing on what we can control and taking determined action, we unlock our potential to overcome obstacles and achieve our goals. In every difficulty, there exists a path forward where perseverance leads to triumph.

#80 

*Life is 10% what happens
and 90% of how you react to
it.*

- Charles Swindoll

WISDOM WORDS 80

Wisdom lies in understanding that while we may not always control external events, we possess the power to shape our responses. This quote emphasizes the significance of our attitudes and choices in navigating life's challenges. By focusing on our reactions with resilience, positivity, and adaptability, we harness the majority of our influence over our own experiences and outcomes.

#81 ☆

Brains aren't designed to get results; they go in directions. If you know how the brain works you can set your own directions. If you don't then someone else will.

- Richard Bandler

WISDOM WORDS 81

True wisdom lies in understanding the intricacies of the mind. Rather than passively letting thoughts dictate our course, comprehension empowers us to guide our own paths. By grasping the workings of our brains, we assert control over our destinies, avoiding manipulation by external forces and steering toward fulfillment and purpose.

#82

Wisdom comes from experience, but experience is not enough. Experience anticipated and experience revisited is the true source of wisdom.

- John Grinder

WISDOM WORDS 82

This quote emphasizes that wisdom isn't merely gained from going through events; it's about reflecting on those experiences. Anticipating situations and revisiting past encounters with a critical eye allows for deeper insights to be gleaned. True wisdom emerges from a continuous cycle of learning, applying, and reflecting on life's lessons.

#83 

I am not the product of my circumstances. I am product of my decisions.

\- Stephen Covey

WISDOM WORDS 83

This quote underscores personal agency and responsibility. It emphasizes that one's character and trajectory in life are shaped more by the choices made in response to circumstances rather than the circumstances themselves. It empowers individuals to take ownership of their lives, acknowledging that their decisions ultimately determine their path and outcomes.

#84

Silence is essential. We need silence, just as much as we need air, just as much as plants need a light. If our mind is crowded with words and thoughts, there is no space for us.

- Thich Nhat Hanh

WISDOM WORDS 84

This quote emphasizes the profound significance of silence in nurturing our inner selves. Like air for breathing and light for plants, silence is vital for mental clarity and inner peace. When our minds are cluttered with incessant noise, there's no room for reflection or deeper understanding. Silence provides the space for introspection and connection with our true essence.

#85 

Awareness is like the sun,
when it shines on things,
they are transformed.

- Thigh Nhat Hanh

WISDOM WORDS 85

This quote highlights the transformative power of awareness. Much like the sun illuminates and alters our perception of the world, awareness brings insight and understanding to our experiences. By shining its light on our thoughts, emotions, and surroundings, awareness enables growth, healing, and a deeper connection to ourselves and the world around us.

#86 ☆

What you think, you become.
What you feel you attract.
What you imagine your
create.

- Buddha

WISDOM WORDS 86

This quote emphasizes the power of thoughts, emotions, and imagination in shaping our reality. It suggests that our mental focus influences our experiences and outcomes. By cultivating positive thoughts, feelings, and creative visions, we align ourselves with the energies we wish to manifest, ultimately shaping our lives in profound ways.

#87

Meditation is ultimate mobile devise; you can use it anywhere, anytime, unobtrusively.

- Sharon Salzberg

WISDOM WORDS 87

This quote highlights meditation's versatility and accessibility, likening it to a portable tool for inner peace and clarity. Unlike physical gadgets, meditation requires no external equipment, making it effortlessly adaptable to any setting or situation. Its unobtrusive nature allows for seamless integration into daily life, offering moments of tranquility wherever and whenever needed.

#88 ☆

Realize it deeply that the present moment is all you have. Make the now the primary focus of your life.

- Unkown

WISDOM WORDS 88

This quote underscores the significance of mindfulness and living in the present moment. It urges a profound understanding that the present is all we truly possess. By prioritizing the now, we cultivate a richer, more fulfilling life, fully embracing each moment's opportunities, experiences, and connections, rather than dwelling on the past or worrying about the future.

#89 

Positive thinking will let you do everything better than negative thinking will.

- Zig Ziglar

WISDOM WORDS 89

This quote emphasizes the transformative power of a positive mindset. By focusing on solutions rather than problems, positive thinking enhances creativity, resilience, and productivity. It fosters a mindset of possibility, enabling individuals to approach challenges with optimism and determination, ultimately leading to greater success and fulfillment in all aspects of life.

#90

Believe you can and you're halfway there.

- Theodore Roosevelt

WISDOM WORDS 90

This quote emphasizes the transformative power of belief and confidence. By cultivating a positive mindset and believing in oneself, one has already taken a significant step towards success. It highlights the importance of self-assurance and optimism in overcoming challenges, propelling individuals forward on their journey towards achieving their goals.

#91 

You are never too old to set another goal or to dream a new dream.

- C.S. Lewis

WISDOM WORDS 91

This quote emphasizes the timeless nature of aspiration and possibility. It encourages individuals, regardless of age, to continuously envision new goals and dreams. It suggests that the journey of self-discovery and achievement is lifelong, affirming the potential for growth, reinvention, and fulfillment at any stage of life.

#92

*Optimism is the faith that
leads to achievement.
Nothing can be done without
hope and confidence.*

- Helen Keller

WISDOM WORDS 92

This quote underscores the transformative power of optimism, which fuels our journey towards success. It emphasizes that hope and confidence are essential catalysts for achievement. By maintaining a positive outlook and believing in our capabilities, we empower ourselves to overcome challenges and strive for greatness, driving us towards our goals with unwavering determination.

#93

*The future belongs to those
who believe in the beauty of
their dreams.*

- Eleanor Roosevelt

WISDOM WORDS 93

This quote emphasizes the power of belief and vision in shaping one's destiny. It suggests that individuals who have faith in the beauty and significance of their dreams are the ones who will ultimately shape the future. By holding onto their dreams with conviction and determination, they pave the way for their realization.

#94

Self-love, self-respect, self-worth: There's a reason they all start with 'self.' You can't find them in anyone else.

- Unknown

Wisdom Words 94

This quote emphasizes the importance of self-empowerment and internal validation. It highlights that fundamental aspects like self-love, respect, and worth originate within oneself. Seeking them externally is futile; true fulfillment comes from cultivating a positive relationship with oneself. It encourages individuals to prioritize their own growth and well-being rather than seeking validation from others.

#95

*Believe in yourself and all
that you are. Know that
there is something inside you
that is greater than any
obstacle.*

- Christian D. Larson

WISDOM WORDS 95

*This quote underscores the power of self-belief
and inner strength. It encourages acknowledging
one's inherent potential and resilience. By
recognizing the innate capacity within oneself to
overcome challenges, it instills confidence and
determination. Embracing self-assurance,
individuals can navigate obstacles with courage,
knowing they possess the resources to triumph
over adversity.*

#96 

---

*Love yourself first and
everything else falls into line.*

- Lucille Ball

WISDOM WORDS 96

This quote underscores the foundational importance of self-love in fostering a balanced and fulfilling life. By prioritizing self-care and acceptance, we cultivate a strong sense of worthiness and inner peace. This, in turn, harmonizes our relationships, choices, and experiences, as we approach them from a place of genuine self-respect and compassion.

#97

You yourself, as much as anybody in the entire universe, deserve your love and affection.

- Buddha

WISDOM WORDS 97

This quote emphasizes the importance of self-love and self-compassion. It reminds us that we are worthy of our own affection and care, regardless of external validation or circumstances. By recognizing our inherent value and treating ourselves with kindness, we cultivate a sense of worthiness and inner peace essential for personal growth and fulfillment.

#98

It's not what happens to you, but how you react to it that matters.

- Epictetus

WISDOM WORDS 98

This quote underscores the power of perspective and attitude in shaping our experiences. It emphasizes that external events are not as significant as our response to them. By choosing positive, constructive reactions to life's challenges, we retain agency over our emotions and actions, ultimately influencing our overall well-being and growth.

#99 

The greatest glory in living lies not in never falling, but in rising every time we fall.

- Nelson Mandela

WISDOM WORDS 99

This quote illuminates the true essence of resilience and triumph. It emphasizes that our greatest achievements stem not from avoiding failure, but from our ability to persevere and rise stronger after each setback. It underscores the transformative power of resilience, turning adversity into opportunities for growth, learning, and ultimately, greater success.

#100

Success is not final, failure is not fatal: It is the courage to continue that counts.

- Winston Churchill

WISDOM WORDS 100

This quote emphasizes the transient nature of success and failure. It suggests that success doesn't guarantee permanence, nor does failure signify the end. Rather, it's the courage to persist despite outcomes that truly matters. By embracing resilience and determination, individuals navigate the ebbs and flows of life's journey, continually striving towards their goals.

ABOUT AUTHOR

- *Dipaali Ghanshyam Patel is a dedicated life coach, inner wellness advocate, and author passionate about transforming lives through mental health and happiness. Having overcome her own struggles with low self-esteem, negative thinking, and limiting beliefs, Dipaali discovered the power of continuous learning, meditation, and affirmations in reshaping her subconscious mind.*
- *Her personal journey from feeling unloved and unsupported to achieving*

profound personal breakthroughs inspires her mission to help others unlock their potential. Through her books, workshops, and online courses, Dipaali offers practical tools and techniques to identify and eliminate subconscious limiting beliefs, empowering readers to create positive, fulfilling lives.

- *With a commitment to promoting mental well-being, Dipaali teaches the art of meditation and the science of affirmations, guiding individuals to train their subconscious minds for lasting success and happiness.*

- *Visit her website www.dipaali.life and Join Dipaali on a transformative journey to harness the power of your mind, overcome challenges, and design a life filled with joy and prosperity. Let her experiences and insights be your roadmap to a brighter, more empowered future.*

MY BOOKS

Scan here to read.

9 Secrets of Subconscious Mind

for Manifesting the Desired Outcomes

Scan here to read.

Rewire Your Beliefs

Eliminate Limiting Beliefs, Stop Negative Thinking, Use Empowering Affirmations, and Transform Your Mind.

Scan here to read

Secrets of Happy Life

Conquer Your Inner World with Positive Self-talk.
Master the Art of Forgiveness and Experience Joy.
Fill Your Heart with Love and compassion.

Scan here to read

Everyday Happiness

21 Tiny Habits to Conquer Your Stress,
Experience Joy and Have a Content Life.

Scan here to read

Secrets of Happy Family

7 Timeless Principles to Cultivate Love, Deepen Understanding, and Perpetuate Mutual Respect Among Loved Ones.

Scan here to read

Workbook - Practice to Be Happy

66 Quick Prompts to Transcend Sadness, Embrace Happiness, Unveiling the Secrets to Lasting Joy.

Scan here to read

Instant Happiness Quotes

100 Powerful Thoughts to Empower Self-Confidence, Cultivate Resilience, and Illuminate the Path to Joyful

Scan here to read

Unlock Your Subconscious Mind

5 Steps Formula to Conquer Negative Beliefs, Foster Positive Change, and Manifest the Desired Outcome Faster.

BIG ASK

Visit my website and join my community for a transformative workshop that is ongoing and upcoming, where we will together spread INNER Purity into the outer world.

I kindly ask you to rate and write a review as an act of kindness. Your review holds importance to me and will positively impact humanity.

Rate and review my google profile

Google/Dipaali-life

www.ingramcontent.com/pod-product-compliance
Lightning Source LLC
Chambersburg PA
CBHW071038250726

48653CB00005B/1881